T0086050

Walk With Me

Walk With Me

POEMS

Madeleine May Kunin

GREEN WRITERS PRESS | Brattleboro, Vermont

Copyright © 2023 Madeleine May Kunin

All rights reserved. No part of this book may be reproduced in any
manner without written permission except in the case of brief quotations
included in critical articles and reviews.

Printed in the United States

10 9 8 7 6 5 4 3 2 1

Green Writers Press is a Vermont-based publisher whose mission
is to spread a message of hope and renewal through the words and
images we publish. Throughout we will adhere to our commitment to
preserving and protecting the natural resources of the earth. To that
end, a percentage of our proceeds will be donated to environmental
activist groups. Green Writers Press gratefully acknowledges support
from individual donors, friends, and readers to help support the
environment and our publishing initiative.

Giving Voice to Writers & Artists Who Will Make the World a Better Place

Green Writers Press | Brattleboro, Vermont

www.greenwriterspress.com

ISBN: 979-8-9883820-5-8

COVER ART:
Emily Mason (1932-2019), Equal Paradise, 1966,
oil on canvas, 48 x 42 inches (121.9 x 106.7 cm).
Image Courtesy of Emily Mason and Alice Trumbull Mason Foundation
©2023 Emily Mason and Alice Trumbull Mason Foundation/Artist Right
Society(ARS), NY

PRINTED ON RECYCLED PAPER BY BOOKMOBILE.
BASED IN MINNEAPOLIS, MINNESOTA, BOOKMOBILE BEGAN AS A DESIGN AND TYPESETTING
PRODUCTION HOUSE IN 1982, AND STARTED OFFERING PRINT SERVICES IN 1996.
BOOKMOBILE IS RUN ON 100% WIND- AND SOLAR-POWERED CLEAN ENERGY.

Contents

II

III

IV

Walk With Me

"Walk with me.
Get your hat and coat
and walk with me."

I heard the words sung
this afternoon during
a folk music concert.

They were seductive,
"Walk with me,"
through the woods,
along the sea, up the mountain,
"Walk with me."
"Yes, I will."

I

Aunt Berthe's Pin

My pin had a yellow oblong gem in the center,
set in filigree silver.
It had belonged to my Aunt,
was given to me after she died.
She wore it often, pinned to her breast.
The clasp was old fashioned, unreliable,
I learned when I raised my left hand to my lapel
at the train station.
It was gone,
people were rushing past me. I was asked by my
    friends,
"Do you want to go back?"
"No," I said, thinking I could adjust to loss quickly.
Besides, there was no hope
of finding it in the railroad car,
or the station packed with multitudes.
So many years have passed, perhaps twenty or more,
that I continue to mourn
the loss of Aunt Berthe's pin,
that fit so well under my throat or on my shoulder.
I have searched for its likeness in jewelry stores
everywhere, but could not find anything like it
    anywhere.
Once I was seduced by a fake yellow stone
and paid one hundred and fifty dollars

for a pin, I thought would satisfy me.
It mostly stayed in its cotton lined box
protected from the light.
Once in a while, even now, I take another look
in a jewelry store, just in case.

Catskills

It was already dark that summer in
front of the Catskills hotel
where we spent two weeks
in a rooming house.
I must have been fifteen, having a crush
on a boy named Frances
without telling anyone.
I stood there with my mother
at ten o'clock that night
in the dark hotel entrance.
We saw her
at the same time
the brilliant yellow light
punching out the dark,
exposing the car with the square roof,
the door held open by him,
for her.
She, must have been
around my age, pretty,
Her leg raised high
to step inside.
The boy at her side
shut the car door
behind her.

A girl, a boy, a car, at night.
Alone, in the dark
my mother frowned.
I held my breath.

Two Grandmothers

I read about a woman who wrote a book
about her two grandmothers.
I did not know either of mine.
A loss I did not feel deeply
until now.

I piece them together from
snippets of stories my mother
gave me.

My grandmothers were each clever
at keeping their families together.

How old was my father's mother,
Babetchen, when her husband died?

I don't know because my father wasn't
there to tell me.

I do know that she managed a store
and took care of her five children, my father
being the oldest, and possibly, her favorite.

Her two oldest sons took care of her
in her old age and moved her to Frankfurt.

The portrait of my mother's mother, Aline,
is more complete.

Both my mother and Aunt Berthe spoke
of their parents with reverence.

"Aline *seelig,* Papa *seelig,*" (blessed) they recalled
acknowledging their souls.

My grandmother had the business sense and
designed some clothing, was *Tuchtig* (capable).

I wish I had known her and my grandfather, Gaston,
I did not know either one.

She would have taught me how to sew instead
of Mrs. Dreyfus in our building in Forest Hills.

I should be grateful for Mrs. Dreyfus, who
let me embroider a silk nightgown for my mother
and gave me a pattern for a felt pocketbook.

Both grandmas must be in my DNA
where I can't see them.

My father's father is blank. My mother's
father was a *luft mensch*—his head in the clouds

and his feet were in politics.
He is closest to me or I to him.
I have no memory of my grandparents
but their energy goes round and round
inside me without making me dizzy.

It Grows Dark

It grows dark before I am ready
to turn on the light under a
smudged sky
spanning above my head.

Splinters of faded blue
push through this tufted quilt.
Oh, for the return of the yellow sun—
Gushing with light

—spilling all over the place
until nine o'clock at night.
Now earth turning
Now sun shadowed
throwing light on someone,
somewhere,

While I wait.

It's been over a year since you died.
I feel better now, in some ways.

Shovel full, by shovel full

Kaddish

My father died when I was two and a half,
some eighty-five years ago.
I work hard to picture him alive
so I can mourn him on the
anniversary of his death,
and recite Kaddish, according to law.

Photographs, some brown, some black,
are the only leavings of his life
small swatches that I try to sew together
into a garment that fits his elegant pose.

He was a miser with memories,
and with his love for me.
If he had really loved me,
would he have killed himself
by sliding over the side of the rowboat
and letting himself slip into
the blue waters of lake Zurich?
Was it sunny on that day, July 31, 1935?

I like to think that the lake sparkled.
That the first gulps of water tasted fine

quenching his tortured thirst.
When did the water turn black?
When was he retching for air?
When did his feet scream?

Laundry

That morning I hung out freshly washed diapers
    to dry
in the sun-scarce alley way, in the back of our building
in Cambridge, Massachusetts.
When I took them down that afternoon,
I pressed my nose into the folds
that smelled like freshly cut grass,
never mind the gray sidewalk.
I laid the diapers in my wicker basket
where a small black cinder had fallen from above.
I picked up the diaper and shook the cinder off
before I neatly laid the diaper down again.

Mother-Daughter

We talk like girlfriends, sometimes.
I forget she's my daughter, when
we share small secrets
about the women and men
who bump into our lives.
When I forget
for a spasm
the difference,
I am as young as she is.
But she usually stops me
in time, before I over reach
and forget my motherly place,
caught deep in love.

I still see her becoming,
some green buds wound tight
with expectation, even now
that she is getting old, almost like me.
She was curled in my womb
when I did not know
who she was, or would be.

But I felt her
pushing this way and that.

A living thing.
At one end of our
umbilical cord.

Now that we speak,
mouth to mouth,
we know one each
until we listen closely
and hear other voices
from another room.

Mrs. May's Apple Cake

The once-stiff white recipe card
had been squeezed into
the gray metal box too long.
Now was yellow and soft
like an old linen dish towel
and smelled like dust.

All that pulling the card out
and forcing it back in
had frayed the edges
and folded the corners up.
But the words still spoke;
"Mrs. May's apple cake."
She had called the dough Meurbe Teig,
a name extracted from Alsace,
where they spoke
both German and French.

The card instructed me in English:
Cream a ¼ pound of butter,
Add sugar, one egg
Sift 1 cup flour with ½ teaspoon baking powder,
Oh, I forgot a pinch of salt, too late.

I followed her recipe, more or less.
I scraped out the apple core,

sliced the apples nice and thin,
and layered them in a circle around the dough.

I splashed ½ cup of cream
into a small blue and white bowl,
whisked the cream together with
2 tablespoons of sugar and
one fat egg.

I spilled the mixture over the apples
drowning them in glossy yellow
and slid them into the oven, carefully,
while my mother seemed to be
by my side.

My Son

I looked at my son's face
and searched for my face in his
while we were eating pizza
at the dining room table.

He had made good choices
when he brought pizza home.
One was mushrooms and mild,
the other somewhat spicy,
but not too hot for me.

I should no longer be surprised
that he is a man,
with more gray than I remember
thick, now, above the ears.

He is more angular than
he used to be.
I found part of me in his face
and fell in love with him.

What Was My Mother Thinking

What was my mother thinking,
when she took the tapestry out of its gold frame
folded it twice and laid it in the metal trunk
bound for America.

It never found its frame again.
I could have been married to Hugo
they said, when I was six,
and had children with buck teeth
spooning matzoh ball soup on Friday nights.

Instead, my son cooks a pork roast
for six hours on my daughter's birthday,
and almost everyone at the table said
it was so good.

When I Was Nursing My Babies

When I was nursing my babies,
I sat in an old rocking chair,
back and forth, suck, suck.

I had painted it a pale violet
decorated the sides with vines
in a darker violet.

When my husband and I parted
I forgot to ask for the chair.
Years went by and
I didn't miss the rocking chair.

Years later, when he moved out of the house
he gave me the chair back.
It now is wedged into a crowded corner
of my bedroom
where its feet stick out.

I tend to trip over it
in the middle of the night.
I have not sat in it.
But I must keep it
now, that I have it.

Losing Sleep

When the switch goes off
without me,
I want to lose myself
in mindless dark.

Another hour has passed
while I did nothing except
struggle with Morpheus
and shove the cat to the
other side of the bed.

Dream of Spring

Winter bites my face,
smashing a red blot
against my white cheeks.

A cracking sound underneath
could be an iceberg
sloughing off skin.

My muffler slips from my chin,
I pull it up and hide behind it
already allowing myself

to dream of spring.

"Weltschmerz"

Weltschmerz is the right word
for the weight that presses down

on me, and rounds my shoulders
in this time of pandemic.

Weltschmerz is a German word,
the first language I spoke

with a Swiss dialect.
It is hard to translate.

I break it in half and get
Two words: "world" and "pain."

They cleave together
in a noxious fog

that stings my eyes,
and brings on tears.

Such a global pain is different from other pain
that I can trace back to myself.

Weltschmerz is an encircling sorrow
felt for the suffering of the world.

It is opaque. It is heavy,
Too heavy, by far, to lift alone.

The Past is Crowded with Ghosts

At the dinner table,
I can hear them talking
not catching
all their words.

I imagine they are talking
about who is sick
and who is well,
who is bedridden,
and who is improving;
who died
and who was born.

The thunder of war
sounds overhead.
Go to America!
Who has gone and
will not come back.

A postcard from my grandfather
high waves against the deck,
an iceberg in the distance—
that's what I have of him,
lost in a pile
somewhere in a box.

The Emperor Trio

The bow in her copper-colored blouse became
   undone
with one loose side hanging down to her waist.
Her body, barely hinged to her chair
devoured Beethoven in gulps.
Her head thrown back, bow in the air
as if she were about to attack
a fleeting note, with her obedient violin,
held fast in the grip of her pretty chin.
She smiled at the cellist.
She, too, was enjoying herself.
Digging deep to release her correct notes.
The pianist, sitting slightly apart,
played for them both
pumping notes—both soft and hard—
into an empty space,
wherever it opened wide enough to let him in.
My mind raced madly, to keep to their pace.
The music stopped.
The lights went on.
I still heard the music coarse through my bones
as I clapped.

—II—

Nap Time

I don't want to go to bed.
It's 2:25 in the afternoon.
Good hours ahead to
get something done,
like a poem.
Sleep envelopes me.
I struggle to shake it off.
Just back from a winter walk.
24 degrees Fahrenheit.

That should keep me awake
with my nose running
wiped by a tired Kleenex,
looking at the sky for snow.
It's not just cold air
and exercise I want.
It's insight, wisdom,
a quick surprise,
even about death,
always present.

Only December

It's dark before it is
supposed to get dark.
A layered gray sky
with a few holes
that open to the next layer.
Almost bulletproof.
It's only December.
So many more grays ahead.
Don't hurry.
This is your life.
Chew your food slowly.
Look at your footprints
in the snow.
Swing your arms,
back and forth.
Breathe deeply
and count.

February Light

February light is kinder
than January, with its sharp edges that
cut my cheeks.
February spills like milk over the landscape
washing it clean.
I look at the Turner sky
with its moving parts of
red and rose.
I want to see how the weather
will change, in February light.

Clouds

Clouds are made of concrete
on this windy afternoon.
I feel their March weight.
As I tilt my head back
black clouds brace themselves
against my white, brow
blocking spring dreams
of warmth, of light, of love.

Spring Ice

Weighted snow on red tulips.
Untimely.
Looks like a tender tucking in,
except their backs are curved
bowing helplessly,
as if in abeyance,
to a pitiless ice God.

One, For the First Time

The highway, thick
with Queen Ann's lace,
in weed-like abundance.
Not worth my attention
until I heard her say,
"Aren't they beautiful?"
Then I saw One
for the first time.

Soil

I went to the plant nursery today
to breathe garden growth
and feed on pinks and reds and gold.
Even the soil had a seductive smell,
layers of browns and blacks
heavy, wet and deep, promising growth.
I seek relief from a lazy spring
too exhausted to appear on time.
No sun has cut through
the cardboard sky,
No warmth has touched
my shivering skin.
My thoughts are inward, downward,
until I take my shovel
scoop earth,
and dig my way out.

Hot Weather

"It's pretty hot today,
but there's a breeze,"
I said to my neighbor,
as we passed each other on
the sidewalk.

She was pushing her walker,
when she stopped and said,
"I don't like hot weather."

Such a final statement. Does
she suffer through much of
July and
all of August,
crossing out months
to nearly zero?

Strawberries and raspberry

Strawberries and raspberry,
that's how the air smells
after a summer rain.

I breath in deeply
until I am filled up.

Summer's End

At summer's end,
green leaves, shake themselves
red with excitement.
Same as last year,
still a surprise.

Each day must decide
before it reveals itself—
Will it still be summer
or already fall?

The Best-Looking Tomato

Things to remember—
Working at Manganaro's on Ninth Avenue
in New York City.
I was a student
at Columbia School of Journalism,
and needed the money.
I learned how to run
the awesome expresso machine
and toss the grounds out
by tapping on the metal cup
upside down.
I made lots of grinders, all kinds.
One I especially liked,
eggplant with tomato sauce.
Ernesto and I worked behind the counter.
He was always sad,
homesick for Italy.
I felt sorry for him
and made small talk.
At noon the crowd surged in
from the garment district.
I can't remember his name
but I remember how he greeted me,
"You're the best looking tomato on Ninth Avenue."
Also, "You'll be a great authoress," he predicted.

Cooler Weather

The thought of cooler weather
pushed indoors
makes me breath
deeply
into my lungs,
as if it were
the last time.

Certain of the Future

I admired her light-gray sandals, and told her so.
"I got them at Costco, twenty-five dollars.
I bought three pairs, one
for each year."

"One for each year?" I asked myself.
How certain she was
of the future.

Would she live that long,
and would her taste be always
the same?

Three years in a row.
I could not think like her.
I live one year at a time.
I want to
leave room for surprises.

Cover

I am swathed in fantasies
when I pull the duvet
up to my chin.
I enjoy them
like ice cream.

Goodbye 1

She asked me for my arm,
on her right side.
She held her cane on her left.
"I've had operations on both knees,
they're still weak.
I don't want to fall."

I had heard these words for the seventh
or the eighth time that morning.
For her, it was the first time.
I pretended it was my first time, too.
"I just have one brother left," she told me,
with a mournful sadness.

It was not new news to me.

She was tethered to a refrain
coming from somewhere in
her somewhat clogged brain.

She is my sister-in-law,
who I love,
as if for the first time.

She remembers filling stockings for
my children when they were little,

so excited by the early morning surprises,
atouch of Christmas for Jewish nieces and nephews.

You couldn't tell by looking at her
that anything was wrong.
A wonderful smile,
a beautiful woman, still,
with new lines circling her eyes.

A childlike perplexity gives her pause,
"Is that right?" she asks her husband
who is used to telling her what's right.
She cries when we hug good-bye.
I cry too.

I Look at Photos of Myself

I look at photos of myself,
Twenty, thirty, forty,
Even fifty years ago.
Who was I then,
Simply more of myself?

Stronger bones,
Clearer voice,
Higher step?
Ambition already chiseled on
stone?

Or was I a different person, then
With water color lines that
Could swim this way or that
Depending on
My inclination.

Or was the design already firm
In my thirties, forties and fifties?
Leaving me helpless, like
A leaf in a downward stream?

In my old age, I'm curious about
Who I was then, and who
I might have become.

What if I had paused
At a tangle of sticks,

Forced to take
A roundabout turn.
Then, what?

I Look Forward to My Bed at Night

I look forward to getting into my bed at night,
fluffing up three pillows,

Covering myself up
with the expensive duvet,

all the way up to my chin,
ready for sleep.

The first few minutes hold promise.
I find a comfortable position

that will let me ease from
consciousness to nothing.

But my position is still not right.
I turn to the left, hug myself

and pull the covers tight
over my hunched shoulder.

Not right either.
I turn in the other direction

pawing at the bottom sheet
to lift my weighted body

to a better place
where it may float

like seaweed
on the surface of the ocean.

I had begun with soft yawns
tolerant of time spent,

now time
has made me angry

at myself, the pillows, the covers,
even the rumpled sheets.

I cannot, will not,
reach oblivion

until daylight wakes me up
and I am pleased.

Isolation

My feelings are hurt
when my cat doesn't
come up to my bed
when I am ready
to go to sleep.

Doesn't she love me at night
as much as during the day
when she wedges herself
between my thigh and the end of my sofa,
waiting to be stroked?

When I am almost asleep,
I suddenly feel her four paws
pressing down on my shoulder
and indenting my stomach.
I am happy to feel her intrusion.

Should I turn to my left side or my right?
Asking the cat for permission
—this sounds so silly,
during this time of
isolation.

III

Earring

I keep losing one earring.
Sometimes I find it again
And feel like
I fell on buried treasure.
I lost that gold circled one
That I got from the museum.
I'm sure they don't make it anymore.
That's the same one that
Fell down the sink with a plunk
On the closed compactor.
I would have torn it to pieces
If I hadn't fished it out
By my clumsy finger tips.
—Happily
And promptly put on two earrings
Where they belonged.
Only five minutes later,
The wandering earring
Fell off again.
I've been scouring the floor
The rug, down my neck
Even inside the toilet
For that glint of gold
—Ever since.

Eighty-seven

Preparing for eighty-seven.
I don't have time to waste
to go down the drain,
like waste water, into the sea,
swirling with the rest.

Eighty-nine

I am eighty-nine,
hovering below ninety,
which scares me.
Undeniably close
to losing everything
that holds me together.

My knees, my teeth
my head that plays
hide and seek with words.

Can I write,
I wonder?
Can I love?
What shall I do, beyond exist?
Live!

Dreams

Last night I dreamt I couldn't climb the ladder
from the lake to the dock.

Was it real or a dream?
It kept me awake.

I couldn't scale the last rung
of the ladder; slippery and steep.

My body was as dense as clay,
my legs loaded with chains.

I was stuck on the third rung
fell backwards,

hitting the water hard.

Failure left me bent over
with shame.

The next day, the dream
still fresh in my mind,

I walked down the ladder
finding each rung

where it should be.
So easy.

Time to go up.
Rhythm moved me,

one, two three—
now the last rung—

I raised my right leg,
gathered my strength,

bounced on to the deck,
and stood tall.

Hoarding

The clerk at the hardware store
met me in the parking lot, curb side.

Bird seed, he brought it out,
a shopping cart full

The fat bags leaning over the side.
I was embarrassed.

To put him at risk
in the midst of Covid

I had ordered three twenty-five pound bags
without knowing how big they were

Or how heavy
I couldn't lift them either into or out of the trunk.

Helpless, I asked the healthy looking young man,
Can I exchange them for five or ten pound bags,
    please?

He obliged, unaware that he was risking his life for
    the birds
I could not, would not, run out of birdseed.

I Cannot Sleep

Which is better,
left or right?
I search for the perfect pillow
with the right indentation,
without disturbing the cat.

I want her here,
taking the place of you.

I cannot sleep

I seek the lake
I stroked last summer
water slipping off me
seamlessly.

I seek the blue sky
seasoned with clouds
I am halfway there,
no further.

I am awake.
I want to paste my body
to the bottom sheet
into oblivion.

I turn to the other side
which looks better
for my head.

I search for the moment when
I give up and disappear
and lose myself
in mindless dark.

I look for where to leave my legs
They must rest somewhere.
I fold into a fetal position
my knees close to my chest
and count to ten slowly.
Deep breaths.

I can only count to nine
and lose interest.
Another hour has passed
while I did nothing except
struggle with Morpheus and
shove the cat to the other side of the bed.

My Cat Loves Me

My cat loves me.
She tells me so.
before I fall asleep,
she climbs up to my bed
and settles herself at my elbow,
beneath the book I hold up high.
She purrs like a cello
her eyes in a heavy slant
trusting me to stay still
until something stirs her
and she picks herself up
and silently leaves.

Tremor

My hand shakes too much
from a tremor,
my doctor told me it was
an Essential tremor.
Not essential to me.
It is not a prelude
to Parkinson's,
or something totally destructive,
equally bad, that would kill me.
Now it's gone.

How could it slip away so fast?
When will it come back?
Too many words dissolve
on my tongue before
I can articulate them.
Too many holes in my head
that the air blows through,
quietly.

The Vein

The vein on the surface of my right arm
protrudes
like a lanyard
woven at summer camp.
A square pain runs midway
down from my shoulder.
I held out my left arm
to compare.
No sign of bluish vein.
Smooth as a gloved arm.
I raised my right arm high
in the air
to tell the blood to slide down.
I moved my fourth finger back and forth
to get rid of the cramp,
clamped and unclamped my hand
if it was the onset of a stroke, I
didn't remember if my heart
was on my right side
or left.
Would it make a difference?
I went back to the evening news
forgot about it, almost,
until I turned on my bedside light.

The swelling had receded,
my hand no longer cramped.
I will live, after all
after fearing
I was about to die.

The Knife

He sliced me down the middle
to grab my angry bowel,
the small one
I was told.
How did he untangle the knot
push and pull,
or just cut through
with his glistening knife?
And then reach for the gun
and shoot it at my belly,
twenty-four small staples
all neatly in a row,
good work.
There must have been blood.
Lots of it.
I did not see a drop.

At the Eye Doctor

I sat in the ophthalmologist's waiting room
for two and a half hours,
with my New Yorker magazine,
that I could not read because
my eyes were dilated.

I could not see.
But I could think
about all this wasted time
spent sitting in a chair
looking at other patients,
wondering who would be next.
When would it be my turn?
Don't they understand, I don't have time to waste!
I am old.

I focus on what patients are wearing:
their sneakers and socks,
their hair, their hands, their eyes.
Meanwhile, I rehearse how I would complain
to the doctor, to anyone about
how badly they managed the system.
It was for the convenience of the doctor,
not the patient.

I would explain we were helpless,
shifting for hours in our chairs

staring at every nurse who
walked by, hoping we would be next.

The door opened,
the smiling doctor walked in.
"Hi, Madeleine," he exclaimed.
"How is your son Adam?"
"Fine," I said and smiled back.
I forgot every word
I was going to say.

It's been over a year since you died

I filled you in,
level with the earth,
that contained mounds of memories.

I remember sailing up the Nile
seeing a farmer standing on the shore,
ancient ruins behind him
still standing there for us.

I remember walking around Saint Victoire
inhaling lavender in France
while slipping on small yellow rocks.

I remember opening the balcony door
of our fourth floor Paris hotel room
and looking down at the lavender trees below.

I remember walking up to the top of the street
and discovering the Arc de Triomphe,
so close.

I remember the sweet sound of
bells as a parade of sheep
scampered down a path

right next to the hotel,
somewhere in the Lake District.

One year later
I turn the pages of my picture book
and find you there.

Answering

I cannot erase your voice
from the answering machine.

I should.
It is time.

No, not now.
Not yet.

I loved your voice
I love it still.

Warm, kind—
even to strangers.

Now I linger,
over your lasting words.

I hover over your photograph
about to speak

about to smile,
as you hold a glass

about to meet
your lips.

You listen to someone
I cannot see,

cannot hear
from my side.

Your V-necked sweater,
light blue, white collar, knotted tie

those white spiky eyebrows.
I would not let you trim

I turn the lamp toward you
to catch your slender pose

Closer, closer, until—
my eyes almost touch

your eyes.

Goodbye II

I knew but didn't know.
All those soft good-byes
when I grew impatient
with your dying.
You worked hard to
reach the end.
In and out. Pause.
In, more slowly.
Out . . . not yet.
Pause . . . counting.
Wait, stop
Gone?
Blood drained,
gray, still.
Untouchable, cold.
I brave a kiss
on your cool forehead,
the only part
I dared to touch,
and make my exit.
I beckon you back
one more time
to pocket my hand,
in yours.
I dared to touch.

Driving

I felt abandoned when the car
in front of me
took a right turn and disappeared.
We had kept a safe distance
between us, for miles.

Moving in and out of lanes, keeping
the identical speed.
We had become partners,
stopping simultaneously
at every red light
starting on cue, when
the light turned green.

Pausing patiently at every yellow.
I didn't need to know the driver,
or the number of passengers, if any.
It was THE CAR I identified with.
As we drove almost in tandem on
this ribboned road
other cars overtook me.
They meant nothing to me,
but when my car
took a right hand turn
without me,
I was bereft.

Slow Spring

First the daffodils die,
then the tulips stiffen,
then the lilacs perfume
turns biter brown and
the peonies slump
to their death.

I mourn them one by one.

A Hand at My Back

There was a hand at my back
when John was alive.
I felt it.
I was loved,
I was saved
from my own footsteps,
his matching mine.
Questions suspended in the air
caught by him and returned,
without effort.
I spoke my thoughts out loud
where they landed on his fingertips.
I remember how free I felt
letting go.
Having been loved
made me brave.

The Loon

I want to tell you about
the loon's lingering call.
When I say "loon" slowly
with a long "oo"
as in "moon."
I repeat
"Loon, loon,"
for pleasure.
I listen for its mournful cry from
somewhere on the lake,
I don't know where.
What meaning
has this nearly human voice?
Is the loon screaming "danger" to
her newly hatched chicks?
Could the loon be singing soprano
to her beloved?
When the loon sings to me,
I startle—
So clear a sound
slicing through the air
until it reaches my heart.
I wait in suspended silence
for a second round.

The air remains still
and expectant.
I listen for the memory
of the longing loon
touching every pore of my skin,
before it melts into the lake
and is gone.

Pandemic

In this pandemic
I sleep too much.
9:30, almost 10,
before breakfast.
Too much ice cream at night
like when I ordered
a coffee ice cream soda
at Schrafft's, facing Times Square
with my mother,
when I was fourteen,
looking out the square window
at packs of pedestrians walking by
wishing I could find the boy,
Francis, who I thought I loved,
because he painted landscapes in oils
and played the piano,
drawing my head down
close to the strings.
I wished he would walk me home
from his place to ours,
instead, my mother insisted.

In Lockdown

I am my bare-boned self,
in lockdown,
walled all around.
Dirty white air covering me,
a carapace.
Standing sitting, lying down
all the same; hard on the outside
parched on the inside—
brittle.

I must move
to compose myself
feel pressure at my side
that pushes me awake.

I hear voices
that scramble my head
see shadows down the hall
moving my way.

I am a canvas again
drawn from the outside in.

Reading a Book by the Lake

I bought a book to read while
I sat on the porch
in a green painted rocking chair
with a frayed straw seat,
that sagged in the middle.
I thought I could do both:
Look at the navy-blue lake
and turn the page to chapter one,
but the lake would not let me wander.
It pulled me back before
I reached page two.
I was drawn to the water
by horizontal gravity,
arrested by the sparkle
of what seemed like hundreds
(or was it thousands)
of frenzied sparkling butterflies
hip-hopping on the lake.

The lake demanded nothing of me,
not even my attention
it simply *was*.
I was simply *there*.
I was absorbing some restorative elixir
for the rest of the day, or the
the rest of my life.

— IV —

My Body

My body surprises me,
wearing out here,
rejuvenated there.
I am alive
more alive
than I thought.
Depends on where
I look.

Feelings

I allow my feelings
Unexpected as they are,
To be exposed
In daylight,
Carelessly, almost.
Leaving caution
Lying in a ditch.

Yes, I can see danger.
I'm not a foolish girl.
I am a well-lived woman
Who still loves life.

Flowers

. . . an old-age splurge.

When I was young,
I bought flowers carefully,
Only one bunch, one kind.
They were an expense.

Yesterday I bought plump red tulips
and a pot of tight purple hyacinths.
Oh, Joy!

Untethered Life

Free, untethered
in my old age
more free than I was before,
in a hurry
to get somewhere.
always on time.

Now. i am generous
not counting my time
or my spending money
just in case.

I sometimes splurge
without thinking.
what am I saving for?

Old Age

I am old it's undeniable.
Still, I dream of love,
remembering then,
discovering now.

Breast to chest—
a surprise,
lasting but a moment
so strong, so good.

I want to repeat
your wake up call
but I dare not ask
I have been content

with old-age slumber
at ease with
buried passion,
wishing nothing more,

until . . .

New Place

I'm in a new place
where I double "old" into "old,
old."

Close to hugging ninety
a few years distant
when I dare to
look at the horizon.

Would I walk without
a cane or an arm,
stride forward
at a good clip?

Would I then remember
to twist my neck,
look the other way and
back again?
Back to eighty-two,
or three, or four,
even five.

Then, I would
remember where
I should be and when,
seldom wrong or late.

Now, I check the date
not once
but twice.
First thing in the morning
and again at night.

Sometimes I float in timeless air
not fixed by date or time,
kicking my feet,
seeking ground.

I have reached the double old,
so many years past
so few ahead.

But still I dream
of falling in love
when I close my eyes
turn in my bed
and face the wall
kicking.

Secret Happiness

I didn't think it would happen again,
that I would be drawn into deep friendship

with a man I could talk to
about James Joyce and Elizabeth Bishop,

hold hands with, with pleasure.
I am young, not like the adolescent I once was,

Not quite, but similar.
Astounded by my body

And my secret happiness.

Happiness

I didn't want to tell him,
I was falling in love.
Not with him,
with someone else.
So I said, "I am happy."
"No wonder," he said.
"You can't write poetry."
I laughed generously,
delighted to have been caught
in the act of
not writing.

Really Old

Who would have thought
that I could fall in love
when I became really old.
Eighty-eight.
And even beautiful so he said.
He felt erotic
at eighty-four.
I felt—how shall I say it?
awake in every pore.

A New Love in Old Age

A new love
in old age.
How can that be?
I am young
open to him
surprised at myself,
saying *yes, yes*
like Molly Bloom
wearing hyacinths
in my hair.

Egg

He gave me a thimble sized
bird's egg,
robin's egg blue,
found on the gravel path.
A careless thief.
Liquid life oozing
still from a hole
in the robin's egg blue.

Comfortable

We're comfortable together.
He tells me about his day
and I talk about mine.
It has become easy
to sit at the dining table
eating our Take Out dinners
comparing what we chose
from the menu.
Acting like old friends,
which we are not quite.
We are
fairly new at being together
almost a year.

It seems longer.
I love not having to
be cautious with my words.
Letting them come out
however they wish
knowing I'll be understood.
When it's time for him to go
we hug
tightly
kiss more than once.

Tell Everyone

Part of me wants to tell everyone,
including my dentist, today.
I have a close male friendship
and I think I am falling in love.

Part of me is secretive,
I must be careful, and tell only a few,
like my children,
who are happy for me,
and one or two close women friends.

After all, this may dissolve, disappoint.
One of us may die within a year.
I am amazed at what is happening to me,
but I can't shout,
not yet.

Slice

My sharp knife has severed
a slim slice of your gooseberry pie
from the round crust,
still oozing
out at the sides and placed on
a slippery white plate
painted with tiny flowers,
Pretty.

You dolloped on vanilla ice cream
making a delicious flood.
You're a wonderful baker,
I praised, more than once.
Making sure you
heard.

The two pieces were the same,
One for you,
One for me.
Perfect.
That's all I want, I said,
For now.

Words

I attach myself to your words
like lichen
settled on the rough bark
of a host tree.

You signed with "Love."
Only a formality
nothing more,
I say.

My eyes seek night.
My body sinks.
I feel
your touch.

Fully Alive

I gave two TV interviews today,
one in the morning
live on Church Street
in front of City Hall.
Three minutes,
tightly packed
at seven thirty a.m.

The second on Zoom,
that afternoon,
at home, in my study.

Words flowed flawlessly
on to the screened square,
celebrating the 19th amendment

one hundred years ago. Finally,
women could vote. My mind was
fully awake, puffed with success,
free from caution.

Ladder

When I climb up the ladder
on to the dock,
stones in my pockets
weigh me down.
I am old.

When I go down the ladder
my feet find each rung
before I hit the water.
I am young.
The water is mountain cold
I do the side stroke,
the breast stroke
as best I can,
happily,
weightlessly,
avoiding the ladder
for as long as I can.

Second Time Around

I decided to read the book again
because the prose was so thick
it deserved more than one go-around
to untangle.
Surprise!
Second time around,
the words were virgin,
printer's ink unsmudged.
I turned the page.
Had I really read this before?
Yes.
I admired the writer
with awe and envy.
Chewing on each word,
enjoying the taste.

How could I have lost the words so fast?
The first time I had told the world
how great the book was.
The second time around,
how great the book is.

Lost and Found

I looked under the bed first
for my hearing aid.
It might have fallen off
when I put my earrings on
too dark to see much under
the bed, except for
crumpled Kleenex.
The silver piece that fit
behind my ear
would have glinted.
It would have announced itself.

I looked further in unlikely places.
Just in case.
Behind the toilet bowl,
in the waste basket,
covered by piles of papers?

Under the pillows in
the living room?
Next to my computer.
Amidst pens that no longer wrote.
On the bedspread, perhaps?
In case it dropped when
I had been making the bed.

Under the dining room table,
dropped while eating dinner—
I moved the chairs and looked
more than once, and
once again and again.

Losing the hearing aid
was worse than losing an earring
like I had done the day before.
The hearing aid was part of my body.
I was lopsided with just one
in my left ear.
I was almost deaf, oblivious
to what was happening around me.
I had to find it.

I talked myself into believing
I could replace just one hearing aid
and it would not cost
thousands of dollars,
like I feared two hearing aids would,
after my third round of searching
both the house and my car,
I called the Luce hearing center
to find out how long it would
take to get one new hearing aid.
And God forbid, what would it cost?

Stephanie was not in.
Leave a message, I was told.
I did, trying not to sound foolish.
Having gotten that close
to spending a fortune to buy a new one,
I retraced my steps once more.
I stopped for the fourth time at the small hallway
    table
where I kept face masks and
winter hats.

I picked everything up with my two fingers,
one by one and shook it.
A tiny silver triangle hung from a string on a mask
"Oh," I sang. Laughter bounced inside me.
For the first time,
I had found
the secret source of happiness:

Lose something precious, like a diamond ring,
or a hearing aid,
look for it long enough to waste half or a whole day
suffer self flagellation—
when all hope is gone—

you find it.

Siren Cities Call Me

San Paolo, Singapores, Abu Dabi.
I fly high.
Glossed diamonds drop
behind me.
Silver mist
runs past me.
Stumbling clouds are
chopped to pieces
right in front of me.
Blue-eyed sky is scooped clear
white bedding settles below.
When are we going to get there?

Two Weddings

Two weddings in one month
I mothered both brides,
from political infancy onward
and they rewarded me by
giving me a place in the recitation
of their sacred vows.
Each more beautiful than the other
wherever my memory fastened
at one moment or another.
One bride, glowing like moonlight,
the other bride, like sunlight.
Love brushed the cheeks
into a powdery rose, of one.
Love pulled back the hair,
falling like water,
down the back
of the other.
I should not make the two brides alike,
they were not the same
except each had become
drunk on love's good wine
which forced their lips apart.
and their hands to join
with their newly sworn husbands.

I was seated a row apart,
believing what I saw.
and I was about to cry,
for happiness,
for beauty
for promise,
for looking back
on my loves.

Women's Lunch

We talk and talk, on the deck
on a summer afternoon.
It isn't gossip.
No secrets.
It's plain good talk
while we sip iced tea
and eat chicken salad,
lettuce leaves still slippery
with olive oil and vinegar.

We sit at a round table
perfect for four
under a red umbrella,
shaded
from the August sun.
Small intimacies hold us together.
We shower comfort
on a new widow.
A husband with cancer
gets new medication.

We agree with her hope.
We, too, want to save him.

We go back to our past
that is so much longer
than our future.

So many things are funny now,
as we retell our stories
and split with laughter
before we say goodbye,
feeling good.

Writing Poetry

When I write poetry, I am in a dark place.
It's not a cave, or a castle, or a dome,
or a place with sides, or a roof, or a floor.

It's not filled with smoke.
I could tell if it were.
My throat would
spit out a cough.
Ny hand would clap over my mouth
quick as a trap.
I would see shapes—
circles and squares and triangles
falling into each other to find their place
lined up in a row,
ordering themselves
in one line, or two or three.

I wish I could tell you more
about how words come my way.
Writing is like dreaming.
What remains are wisps
that float my way
and then fade into liquid form
like melting ice.

Schedule

I don't like to have blank spaces on my calendar,
not large ones,
too much time to fill—
With what?

But then I don't like it,
when there are too many scribbles,
for a certain date in July,
when I can't read my writing.
Who on earth is "Kathleen?"
Was I to meet her for lunch or coffee?
Too many dates on one day,
I feel pressed, worried that I
won't get where I'm supposed to be.

I didn't look at Friday's email until noon.
"This is to confirm our lunch at 12:30."
"Oh, my God," it's today!
I had made another lunch appointment
at the same time, plus
I had leant my car to my daughter.
"Quick, call!"
Joan's telephone has been disconnected.
I don't have her new number.
I reply to her email and apologize.

A muddle-minded old woman.
"Come over to my place," I suggest,
trying to make amends,
hoping she will say "Yes."
When I assure her I live close by,
she agrees.

Meanwhile, I search for my other lunch date
in the Wake Robin dining room.
He's there, waiting.
We had joked about forgetfulness
many times before.
Now it was serious.
"No problem," he says,
"but you owe me,"
"Yes, yes,"
I say, turning pink
knowing he was only half joking.

After, I shuffle things around
on my now-messy calendar,
canceling the cleaning women
scheduled for 1 p.m.,
just in time for lunch.

We settle down at my dining table.
Joan is gracious, I am wretched.
(She, having brought the sandwich
she had ordered in the restaurant
while waiting for me; I retrieved
a day-old half sandwich from
my refrigerator.)

I ease up on my self-torture,
and am able to talk in sentences.
"This was even better than eating in a restaurant;
we can talk personally," Joan said.
"Yes," I say, quick to agree.
"It is perfect."

Registration

It's time to renew my car registration.
The notice in the mail gave me a choice:
Renew it for one year, or two.
If I renew it for two, I save twelve dollars
I pause and think about Life.
Will I still be able to drive for two more years
Or will I even be alive in two years?
This existential question demands a reply.
I didn't expect to have to decide so soon,
About mortality.
If I die in the first year, after I paid for two years,
I won't get my money back.
That much I know.
But if I renew my registration for one year,
and live for two years, I'll have lost
the discount for the second year.

I agonize too long.
It comes down to basics:
Am I an optimist or a pessimist?
The Department of Motor Vehicles remains dumb.
It offers no advice.

I sleep the sleep of the undecided
I wake up the next morning and say to myself
What the hell,
I'll take a chance.
And write the check for two.

The Perfect Word

I catch words
between finger and thumb
until they slide away.
They play magic tricks
with a tall black hat
held high in the air.
There it is!
I found it!
The perfect word
right in its proper place,
until I click it out,
choose its neighbor,
that I love even more,
until I change my mind,
once again.
This is *it*.

Fear

I am afraid, not for myself,
I have almost arrived
where I was going to go.

I fear for the others.
The children, and
their children,
and those after that,

How will they carry on
in a burning world?
They read the words,
"Do Not Touch,"
nailed to the globe
behaving like toddlers
warned to stay away
from a hissing stove.

I fear water, like never before.
A blind river insists on smashing
everything in its way.
Cars upside down,
dolls without heads.

I fear storms, shore lines
once fastened firm, ripped off
splashing second-floor windows,
forcing red roofs to run away.

I see a farmer standing
before his field,
grown hard as a dinner plate
crushed to dust by drought.

When that day comes,
when my children must move on
to find shade from the sun,
dry dirt away from the rain,
I'll be gone.

But now, as we wait,
I grow afraid,
for them.

Grammy's Hand

"I want to hold Grammy's hand," she said
No lover could have made me swoon,
like she did,

Her words went *whoosh* to my heart.
Three years old, full of chatter, spilling
into our air.

Such power she has, to give
or withhold, leaving me suspended
in anticipation,

until I feel her small hand
surrounded by mine.
While we walk in step,

slowly.

Mantra

I received my mantra today
I can't tell you what it is.
I keep it secret, I don't tell anyone,
I do not write it down,
but I did, just in case.
I repeat my mantra, like I should,
again and again as I walk
in the heavy outdoor air.
Each time I remember my mantra, I experience
a thimble of success that leads
me on to the next one, like
words in a relay race.

I haven't arrived there yet,
where I am supposed to be,
a state of mind, that
that leaves my mind behind.

They tell me I will feel refreshed
like after a plunge in a cool pool.
Reborn, perhaps, more clear eyed
than before,
brushing against wisdom.
I wonder, my mantra, my very own,
Can you take me there?

Stay in the Moment

I wrestle with myself
to stay in the moment.
My mind squirms,
always slipping out of my hold.
Look at the lake,
the tree
even the tennis court,
dull as it is
without players.
It can't keep me there.

Enjoy the present! I shout.
Concentrate, for God's sake.
Imbed the moment.
Crawl inside yourself
stay there for a minute.
Or more.

Ending

I would like to probe deep,
write about life and death,
the meaning of existence.
I should have the answers
by now,
when the end is so near.
I procrastinate.
I tell myself
there is still time
Maybe tomorrow
Or the next day
Or the day after that
to write about the meaning
of life,

The meaning of my life.
Have I made a difference?
Have I been kind?
Have I dropped a coin
into a beggar's hand?
Will I be remembered,
and by whom?
For What?

I'm too tired
No more deep questions, please.
Maybe tomorrow,
Or the next day
Or the day after that.

AUTHOR PHOTO © PAUL BOISVERT

MADELEINE MAY KUNIN, the first woman to be elected governor of Vermont (three terms), was also the U.S. Ambassador to Switzerland and U.S. deputy secretary of education. She has written four previous books and two books of poetry: *Living a Political Life* (Knopf), *The New Feminist Agenda: Defining the Next Revolution for Women, Work, and Family* (New York Times Editor's Choice), *Pearls Politics and Power,* and *Coming of Age: My Journey to the Eighties* (GWP). Madeleine's first poetry collection, *Red Kite, Blue Sky,* was a finalist for the New England Book Award for Poetry in 2022. She is currently James Marsh Professor-at-Large at the University of Vermont, where she gives guest lectures on feminism, and women and politics. She also served on the board of the Institute for Sustainable Communities (ISC), a nongovernmental organization that she founded in 1991, and she launched Emerge Vermont to encourage and support women in politics. She lives in Shelburne, Vermont.